Resili

CW00552337

The ability to re-balance and recover from change or stressful situations

I hope you enjoy this booklet and keep it close as a gentle reminder that although we cannot choose our environment and the things that happen to us, we can choose how we react to them.

Many thanks to Ian White for bringing my ideas to life by painting the pictures I could see so clearly in my head.

Helen Chapman

Concentrate on what you can control

Make a list of the things you cannot control and throw it in the bin. Then make a list of all the things you can do something about and take action.

Make time to stop and reflect

S   Space to relax and reflect

T   Time to think, feel and notice

O   Organise thinking and perspective

P   Proceed

Acknowledge your feelings

Notice how you are feeling on a daily basis. Just by acknowledging your feelings, when all is not well, you will begin to change them. Try describing how you are feeling right now.

Be gentle on yourself

We are often so much harder on ourselves than we are on other people.

Try telling yourself, "It's OK, I am doing the best I can".

Do more of what makes you feel good

You know what makes you feel good. It may be a long soak in the bath, a walk in the park, a quiet evening in with a good book, a run along the beach or something else entirely. Whatever it is for you, make time for it.

Smile and things will look up

Smiling and laughing do amazingly de-stressing things to our bodies. Looking up also makes us feel better – it's very difficult to look up and to feel down. Try looking up and smiling more and notice the difference.

Be proactive

Just by doing something you will change a situation or move it forward.

What action can you take today that will make you feel good?

Prioritise your own needs

Remember, you are important too. Make a list of all the things that matter to you so you can hang onto them when all around you is going crazy.

Think about the outcome you want

If you could wave a magic wand what would you make happen? Just by knowing what you want, you are increasing the chances of it happening.

Notice the good things

We see things not as they really are, but as we choose to see them. Keep a mental list of all the good things you notice each day.

Choose what you let irritate you

Always remember, you have a choice about how you let things affect you. If you are having a good day, don't let anything spoil it. Take a long, slow breath and remember this picture.

Helen Chapman is Managing Director of Pelican Coaching and Development, a company specialising in coaching, team development and inspirational workshops with offices in Yorkshire and Hertfordshire and a network of associates in the UK and the US.

Helen has a passion for finding new ideas to help individuals and teams to be more effective and resilient.

She is an NLP Master Practitioner, Coach and Trainer who lives near Ilkley in North Yorkshire with her partner.

She loves travelling all over the UK and to the US through her work as an Executive Coach and Consultant.

Helen continues to explore creative ways of helping people to discover what they already know about themselves, their ability to perform and their reactions to stress. She also enjoys helping others to learn new techniques enabling them to perform at their best for longer.

Contact Helen at Helen.Chapman@PelicanCoaching.com